Est. 2018

The Poetry Book I

By
Ramsey Wake
&
Angelina Cruzal

For information about permission to reproduce selections from this book, email to ramseywakepermissions@gmail.com

This stuff is pretty boring to write honestly.

Manufacturing by Ramsey Wake and Angelina Cruzal

Book design by Ramsey Wake and Angelina Cruzal

ISBN: 978-0-359-35569-3

The Wake Poetry Incorporation: (not a real incorporation)

_____ (we're supposed to have a website link here, but we don't have one.)

___ (we're supposed to have an address here, but I'm not telling you where I live.)

For all the social media viewers and for business contacting:

Instagram: @Ramseywake

Okay boring stuff is over, let's dive in.

enter with caution, yet confidence,
for the world you are about to be
consumed by is filled with thoughts
of the deepest, darkest valleys,
though, balanced by those of the
highest peaks. you are on a roller
coaster, my friend. while i know, and
am familiar with the brain that these
thoughts were birthed from, i cannot
say where this roller coaster will
lead you. it is different for all.
but one thing i'm sure of is you'll
get off of this ride feeling
something new. enjoy.

— a.c.

TABLE OF CONTENTS

4

THE WILD

Episode .5 (The Sample)

Her messy hair was a visible attribute of her stubborn spirit.

As she shakes it free,

she smiles knowing wild is her favorite color.

It's yours too.

She reminded you that beauty isn't skin deep,

that love is infinite and hope is a place

that lives inside of all of us.

She craved adventure all her life,

but anyone that met her knew she was an adventure all by herself.

I hope you know how much I needed your Wild,

and just how inspired I have become.

May your firework always explode the night's sky.

This is for wild hearts.

Episode 1 (Call of the Wild)

To all the hearts that don't belong anywhere,

arise.

For all the hearts,

unbeating and broken,

scarred but not scared,

naive and not narrow minded.

For the hearts that cry out for neverland

let me inform you that neverland

isn't a land you can never reach,

but rather a land that lands

in the hearts and minds of all of us.

To expressive personalities personifying souls unshaken

and unstirred by common voices

and words trying to control the world,

and they may do that.

They may complete their task

and they may already rule our world under our noses.

But no matter how much of the world they control

they will never control the wild we inherently inhabit.

We are the wild.

We are the free and we cannot be broken by guns.

We cannot be broken by law

but law can be broken by us if we choose

for the law we abide by is a wild random law

created by our own orbicular minds.

Created by our own steady pens

properly placed in places that make sense to us.

Reshape,

remake,

remind.

And repay all that has been made.

But rely on your hand on the wheel that you drive,

for the future is fast approaching,

and what you miss..

you cannot control.

Episode 2 (Side Effects)

Are you experiencing trouble breathing?

Oh, you are

well you should have that looked at

by a professional.

Loss of self control?

An overabundance of thoughts and or dreams?

Do you want to accomplish things nobody has ever tried?

Would you consider your environment to be filled with people who find you and or your dreams to be wasteful?

Are you tired of blending in?

Then I can feel your crying soul

bash against the oppressive walls,

the best I can offer

is if you will let me cry with you.

You begin to glimpse a world

with a sunrise over a calm beach

with warmth that wraps around your heart

and restores purpose in your chest.

If any or all above is true,

let me personally welcome you to the Wild.

And let me thank you

for choosing to show your stripes

and stand out in a world ready to shoot you down for doing so.

You are beautiful

and the Wild wildly accepts you.

you are loved
so live and breathe life into others
even though they don't deserve you.
Shine bright and colorful my star,
you will accomplish great things.
You'll see.

Episode 3 (The Wanderers)

We fickle-hearted dream worshipers.

This world isn't quite sure what to do with us anymore.

Like mountains that long to swim in the oceans,

Like rooted trees

that wish to soar with the birds he meets,

Like the moon

wishing she could be the light of the world.

We always seem to be the opposite

of what we wish we are.

And that can be real problematic

for a wild child

living in a tidy world

being made tidier by the minute,

a billion rows of cubicles simply won't cut it.

And society that worships whatever popular voice tells them to,

I don't think so.

When asked what I want to be when I'm older,

I have no answers for the common population.

"I want to be WILD." I say.

Nobody has answered to that,

because there is no college to study wild.

There is no apprenticeship,

you just wake up one day,

and realize you're not regular.

Your heart beats a different way,

and the common things of life won't cut it.

So I've become a wanderer.

And yes,

this means I chase things I know I cannot catch,

but I know on the way I will catch something.

Something that isn't explainable,

something that isn't supposed to be caught.

I will catch the colors and the lights

that light souls into bright fires,

and become fireworks.

Wander more often,

you might just find what you weren't looking for.

Episode 4 (Station Identification)

WHAT THE ACTUAL BANANAS,

SOMETHING HAS POSSESSED MY BODY

AND IS THROWING A WILD PARTY WITH MY SOUL

UNDER FIREWORKS AND FUNKY CHRISTMAS LIGHTS.

I AM DANCING.

LET ME REPEAT. I. AM. DANCING.

I DO NOT DANCE,

I HAVEN'T DANCED,

IS THIS HOW YOU DANCE?

SOME SMALL PIECE OF ALL THIS

IS AWFULLY FAMILIAR LIKE AN OLD FRIEND,

BUT THESE FIREWORKS,

MY I HAVEN'T SEEN THEM IN SO LONG.

THIS IS A FULL SHOW,

AT LONG LAST HOW I MISSED THESE BRIGHT FACES.

"HEY SONNY, THOUGHT YOU COULD USE A LITTLE HELP.

SEEMS LIKE IT'S BEEN A WHILE SINCE YOU'VE SMILED,

LET'S TAKE A LOOK.

OH YES, THAT SURE IS BROKEN.

LET ME JUST FIX THAT UP,

OKAY THERE WE GO.

SMILE REWIRED.

AH, LOOKS LIKE WE HAVE A FEW BUGS UP NORTH,

SELF CONSCIOUS THOUGHTS,

A BLANKET USED TO HIDE FROM THE WORLD
THAT'S CLEVER NOW I'LL HAND IT TO YOU.
NOTHING A PAIR OF SCISSORS CAN'T SOLVE
THOUGH.
ALSO IT'S ABOUT TIME YOU GOT THE UPDATE,
THERE'S A NEW SYSTEM OUT.
AND THERE YOU GO,
YOU'RE READY TO BLOW,
TAKE IT AWAY."
AND IT ALL MAKES SENSE NOW,
HOW CAN I BE WILD UNLESS I LET MYSELF GO,
UNLESS I FALL OFF THAT EDGE,
UNLESS I DANCE IN THE DARK,
UNLESS I PLOT TO TAKE OVER THE WORLD.
FROM THE SKY TO THE SEA,
TO THE AIR THAT WE BREATHE,
FROM THE DEPTHS TO THE EDGE OF THE STARS,
THIS WORLD IS OURS.
AND OUR WILD WILL RUN LOUD AND FREE.
I DARE YOU TO TRY AND STOP ME,
I WILL DANCE IN YOUR FACE
AND SING TO A TUNE THAT DOESN'T EVEN EXIST.
MY WILD CAN BE AS LOUD AS IT PLEASES,
FOR WE PLAY BY NO RULES.
WE TELL OURSELVES SECRETS THAT NOBODY HAS
EVER HEARD,
AND ONLY WE ARE IN ON THEM.
AND WE ARE GOING TO BE HAPPY,
BECAUSE WHY THE FUCK NOT?

WHY NOT.

BE WILD, BE FREE, BE HAPPY.

THANK YOU.

- RAM VON BITTLEPANTS (A REAL LIFE STORY, NOT A PAID WRITER. HE'S NOT FICTIONAL, NO.)

Episode 5 (Colors)

I am different.

And I am in this weird place

as I try to understand what colors belong to me.

I know I am different from the rest,

nobody can get down to my music or my jams,

nobody watches my movies,

nobody understands my writing.

And from a young age that was always a bad thing,

I must be doing something wrong I thought.

I wanted to be understood,

I wanted to be able to have a conversation and not be terminally awkward.

I dreamed of having talents like others,

as I got older I hated who I was.

I was so poorly different,

I was unsatisfactory to myself

and I figured I let everyone down

that's why nobody notices me,

these are still struggles to date.

But it dawned on me one afternoon

as I stood in one of those peculiar places

that only I enjoy that,

my difference doesn't have to be ugly,

it doesn't have to be uninteresting because i'm told it is,

it doesn't have to wear a gloomy face.

It doesn't have to be wrong,

why can't it be right?

Why can't I live in my weird world?

If it isn't a superpower

to love things that can't be loved otherwise

then I don't know what is.

I am learning to love myself in unique ways

I didn't think were possible yesterday,

I am bright if I say I am,

I am brave if I act so,

strong if I hold myself up.

I am weird if I wish to be

and I love being odd,

look at me strange and I'll laugh for I know my world.

It's filled of fun colors,

dangerously inconsistent music

that fits together

to create a masonic vibration that stirs the soul.

And the king of this world is I.

And i will nurture this world as long as i can,

life is weird so as long as you give me that dazed and confused look, I can remember I am WILD

and you are gray,

take your pick.

Episode 6 (Brevity)

Brevity,

a word used to describe a shortness of time.

The brevity of our human existence lays so short

many of us will perish before we even open our eyes.

We are zombies

living zealous filled lives

pretending that we are conscious.

I picture that to be

the most perfect of all the pretexts.

Because being American

is supposed to be personification of the good life,

the dream life.

Perhaps prosperous prospects

live in the third world and we don't know.

And who do you blame?

You aim your weapon at brevity.

If I had more time I could help,

but life is short so I can't.

People would rather spend their brevity

boosting their own business,

it's always about getting to the top.

But the top you speak of

isn't topographically the top of the mountain

but rather a moonstone you've encountered along the way.

A moonstone being a gem or an eye catcher.

There's so much life we aren't living.

So many breaths we aren't catching.

And we blame brevity for our lack of this and that.

Your fainting heart will fade faster than smothered fire.

Your breaking brain will be boiled by the boisterous.

And you will blame brevity.

If only I was younger, I could be..

you are young.

You are youthfully yoked by your yearning for freedom of oppression. You fail to act on it.

You've failed to set sail on a magical adventure

into a happy and wild place.

It's never too late,

the boat to a new life is open,

all we ask is you bring nothing with you, but you.

You, and your wild.

Episode 7 (Local Lingo)

Anamokato,

to become one with an animal.

This of course comes from the wakeo dictionary.

Probably not one you're familiar with

considering I just made it up.

Yes, I do enjoy in my spare time

forming a language with words that pertain to me much better.

Because I needed a word to describe how I felt

as my dog and I stared into each other's eyes

and he slowly rests his head in my chest

and falls asleep for the night.

Those moments we shared,

his smile saying i love you, my smile saying I love you,

and to that I give you Anamokato.

And you can't tell me there's one better,

as far as I am concerned

that is the perfect word for the feeling.

Lodaze,

a lost or very buried feeling.

There's no word I know of,

to capture the feeling when feelings are unrecoverable.

The feeling you get

when snow tickles the back of your neck

in Times Square on Christmas Morning.

But that was five years ago,

now your parents aren't together as they
were then,

your brother has run away from home and
you,

you feel nothing but emptiness,

you feel a lodaze.

It goes well with the word Perashua.

Perashua is the pursuit of a lost feeling,

trying to bring it home to your soul.

Going back to new york city all alone,

breathing in the smell of gasoline and
asphalt.

It's nothing short of beauty the city
lights.

Your journey is Perashua.

I am WILD enough to let my heart say what
it wants

even if it's just the sounds a baby might
make

before it gets bogged down to a language.

Release yourself,

let your crazy show.

Go Perashua and save your Lodaze.

Have Anamokato if you're into loving pets.

And one last word you should know.

Vastimoza, let your love be known.

The world deserves to know the colors of
your wild wings.

So spread it everywhere you go,

and you will be a Vastimoza walking the street.

Episode 8 (The Seeds)

Planted into the earth,

we are like seeds.

We are on the rise ready to return to life
above ground.

Ready to release our outer cover

and reveal our true colors.

We are wild flowers,

we will reign on the mountains,

rain making us stronger and nourished.

We won't exist we will flourish,

for you never see a wild flower by itself,

our inviting scent will catch the attention
of others

and join this movement

that likely will last generations.

You pull us out by the roots

our poison will drip onto your skin

and make you think twice next time.

Our mission is righteously constructed,

we chase feelings, love, and truth.

We will not blend in,

we won't hold back our crazy because it
deserves to be seen.

Love us or hate us

we will always exist on your favorite walls

like graffiti on the statue of liberty.

Join us,

we are wild and the truth is we all are in spirit.

Our souls yearn to dance in the street,

and feel accepted and loved.

The wild will never be far away,

all you have to know is where to look.

BROKEN

intro

and it was in that hour.
on that day
in that place
at that time
he knew the summer was over
and he would never hold the key
to the only heart
he could bear to love.

broken

the bump in the road,

is never simply a bump in the road.

it's the beginning of an unfortunate string
of events.

your car spins and you lose control,

in your desperate attempt

to save what little happiness you still
hold onto.

the car veers into the other lane,

fatally colliding with the person

that you never imagined would be in your
life.

she was perfect,

and she was beautiful,

but you are about to kill her and yourself.

your car lands sideways,

to your unhappiness,

you're alive.

you can't even stand up,

the depression keeps you glued to the seat
of your car

staring into a blank dashboard,

waiting for a portal to an alternate
universe

to take you away.

the passenger window broke open in the
crash,

you manage to make a leaping effort.

but the jump jolted the car into motion,

and now you are free falling down that cliff.

that cliff you have joked about so much,

the cliff you scoffed at saying

"that'll never be me down there."

but deep down you knew this day was coming for some time now.

you were always so close to losing everything.

you had so little which is why you drove so carefully.

and as you gain velocity falling through the air

some strange voice in your head reminds you

that all of this could be worse,

truly.

she could've found out you loved her.

you could be watching their cute videos,

cuddling up on a couch

watching your favorite movie with dogs

and food that you adore.

you could be on social media

looking at your feed filled with everything but her,

and everything with them.

you could be watching them in public,

really really creepily.

watching how she looks at him

with such joy and pureness.

you could watch how he accepts her love so
gently.

the car crashes abruptly shattering your
arms and legs,

now you have bones sticking out of skin and
blood in your mouth. you're alive and you
would so much rather be dead.

branches collect through the cars windows,

to your surprise the tree is cradling your
car,

like your mother did

before she learned how to hate you so
perfectly.

like your father did

when you were young and mistake free,

those days are long gone.

you look out your window,

the view of a perfectly lush valley

with a golden sunset dropping into the
ocean

brings you momentary peace in this peril,

at least something went right.

like that time you third wheeled with them
at the zoo.

you didn't want to come,

but your whole hearted love for her

makes it impossible to ever say no to her
requests.

your anxiety is throwing a party,

abusing your stomach,

you have chest pains,

you can hardly move your fucking legs.

but while they left you alone to hold hands and order food,

being the perfect people they are,

you saw the chimpanzee,

more importantly he looked at you.

he smiled,

and for that two and a half second encounter,

the world was just fine.

the car wiggles free from the tree.

there was a wedding invite waiting for you when you got home.

the impact of the ground

shatters your spinal cord

as it shoots out of your skull like a firecracker on fourth of july. it's done,

this isn't going to blow over,

but you've known that for some time now,

it was only a matter of time before today wasn't it?

you aren't going.

and in that action she's going to realize isn't she.

you battle whether or not

life is a viable option at this point,

she'll be disappointed in you,

you're disappointed in you.

with any luck this car crash is going to kill you,

but it won't,

that would be too easy.

if it was meant to be it would've happened by now,

you limbless motorless piece of junk,

just go.

suck it up,

at least you won't completely ruin

the only thing that has brought you any kind of satisfaction, gratification, motivation.

firefighters pull you from the wreck,

and place you in an ambulance.

the doctor looks at you,

with bones sticking out of skin,

he says your heart went black,

"you should be dead."

and i say

"i know."

he stops dabbling with his pencil

and gazes into my heart with fire,

but i am immune.

my heart is all ash.

"what is keeping you alive?"

and to this, the answer is simple.

i got out of my gurney,

"i still love her."

you limp out of the car,

pushing the bones back into your body.

and you continue to walk,

the walk of a broken heart.

happily ever after

love is beautiful.

love is a breath of fresh air.

love is ALL you need.

you can eat love drink love bathe in love,

you sleep love,

you breathe love,

fuck love.

the world makes it sound so easy,

find someone,

fall in love with the someone,

and in turn love will be given back to you.

it's not the truth.

happily ever afters only come to prince's who are charming.

i'm not, and the world tells you,

'there's plenty of fish in the sea'

that's great and true.

but what happens when you find ms. someone,

she's beautiful, she's pure, she's a firework.

and you fall in love with her madly in love.

so you tell her how you feel and she reminds you,

love isn't always a two way street.

so you backtrack,

you blame yourself,

you get low.

you don't want to live,

all the color in your heart turns black,

you see the world darker.

love is a follow request on instagram,

it can't be beautiful until it's accepted.

and so i write this today,

my morning was filled with thoughts

of you holding someone else's hand,

kissing his cheek,

holding him tightly.

the sheer panic and anxiety

of opening social media to see you two

cuddling on a couch and i can feel my insides

stabbing my heart it brings physical pain.

my brain whispers to my heart

'its okay it's okay its okay, it's not worth it.'

and through the echo down to the heart

it hears i'm not worth it.

it's a motto that is branded on your heart

and stays for a lifetime.

love isn't beautiful,

love is pain and why would love mingle with pain,

it would be like you and me happily ever after.

the deep dark ocean

the heavy weight of the deep water i swim in

presses on my chest

like a sustained punch to the stomach.

i am a small fish in a big ocean.

nothing bothers me,

at least not with intent.

i am too small to have predators,

i just clean the coral,

swim to new coral,

clean the coral,

swim to new... this is my life,

i focus on breathing.

but recently my vision is askew.

the heaviness of the water

crushes my small body more than usual.

the water has lost its color,

the sun doesn't shine any longer.

i swim and i swim but there is no coral.

the fish here never notice me.

they swim with smiles and they swim happily.

i can't bear a smile anymore.

i wish i knew why,

perhaps the water is just too heavy.

i try to swim up,

not because everyone else does

but it just seems like the right thing to
do.
but i can't.
the water is too heavy.
the water gets more and more black
until now i can't see anything at all.
i've forgotten how to smile at this point,
the heaviness of my chest
presses in to the point i feel like i'm
suffocating.
my eyelids shut and i can't open them,
soon i'll forget how to do that too.
there's no hope at this point,
i drift into the deep dark ocean
until the pressure cracks my gills
and i choke to death.
depression strangled me out of breathing.

a life with no purpose

deceitful lies told by people who enjoy suffering.

child abuse performed by people who adore agony.

suicide for those who can't take it any longer.

and a year ago johnny would tell you

how unfortunate it is to see someone take their life

because who knows what they could've become.

but here he stands.

phone in one hand,

nine millimeter in the other,

and the reality of the situation is more real than he thought.

"what am i doing here?

they say everyone has purpose

but with seven plus billion people

what are the odds i've been overlooked".

it makes sense right?

nobody sees johnny at school,

and the few who see him elsewhere

look down upon him with pitiful eyes.

this is no way to live.

johnny has no song in his heart,

no heat in his chest,

no thought in his head

that isn't filled with darkness.

just a faint beat in his heart

that doesn't even feel like it's because of his own doing.

rather, a causality of a previous love

and passion who he still believes will come home.

we don't understand what it feels like,

we don't get johnny.

to be so empty.

so desperate.

that you throw the last remaining bit of yourself,

your last hope,

hail mary style and when the ball lands you didn't catch it.

the clock runs out,

you check the scoreboard for no reason at all.

the final score,

you have nothing and your competitors,

don't even exist.

johnny played with himself and he lost.

maybe that's what it's been all along.

a desperate attempt to find himself.

maybe he was supposed to find himself you,

in us.

but we never felt the need to help.

now johnny lies his head on the floor,

and an hour later paramedics will find out

the consequences of a broken society,
giving johnny a life with no purpose.

chaos

a symphony of destruction.

a nightmare dreamed by an angel.

the peaceful noise of a quiet forest

meeting a roaring electric guitar.

murder for love,

that's chaos.

chaos is expecting to bite into chicken

but taste a bloody beating heart instead.

everything becomes blurred.

basic guidelines are no longer meant to be followed.

things you've been previously taught

are thrown out of the window in a violent thrust of wind.

i am filled with chaos.

it's been breeding in my bones and muscle fibers

since i was conceived.

my dreams are horrific

gore filled nightmares

that stand as a bloodbath ceremony for my friends.

and i have no power to prevent it.

the helpless feeling

of holding your dead friend's

dismembered head

with a scrap of metal piercing both sides of the skull..chaos.

my thoughts are just a constant fight

between my head and heart.

my heart bitter

because the soul it's drawn to

isn't in love with my brain.

so it beats angrily at the brain

as if in some tearful daze

reminds the heart that it can't change my appearance.

and even if it could

who could love someone so mentally ill.

the heart understands but it shatters to a million pieces.

and when it is put back together

it's a darker shade of black.

it's hard to put up with the madness,

the chaos.

he feeling of being stuck between two options,

the one you tell yourself and the one the chaos speaks.

it seems no matter how hard i try

chaos has become the head of operations in my body.

and as the violins play

their fearsome drone

i sink away..

swallowed by the chaos.

PEACEKEEPERS

INTRO

LET THEM TALK,

LET THEM HATE,

LET THEM RAGE AGAINST WHAT THEY CANNOT
CHANGE.

WE WILL LOVE.

WE WILL FIND PEACE.

WE WILL DO WHAT WE MUST TO MAKE THIS WORLD
A BETTER PLACE.

EVEN IF WE ARE STILL BROKEN INSIDE.

WE WILL NOT FORGET.

WE WILL RIDE.

WE WILL DO IT SIDE BY SIDE.

WE WILL FLY.

SOME OF US WILL SNOWSHINE.

SO BURN YOUR BRIDGES,

AND TORCH YOUR WOODEN SHIPS,

FROM THIS POINT ON,

THERE IS NO TURNING BACK.

FREEDOM RIDER

MAKE WAY QUICKLY.

FOR THE MAN WHO MOUNTED HORSE,

WITH INTENTION TO CHANGE THE WORLD AND ITS COURSE.

TO SET HIS HOME FREE OF CURSE,

EVEN AT THE WORST PUNISHMENT.

HE STUCK HIS FACE TO THE DIRT

AND ALLOWED CAPTORS TO STEP

EVER SO CAREFULLY ACROSS HIS BACK

IN ORDER TO AVOID THEIR FEET FROM BECOMING UNCLEAN.

HE WHO WISHES TO CHANGE THE WORLD

SHOULD NOT HESITATE AT THE OPPORTUNITY

TO STAB A HORNET'S NEST.

SHOULD NEVER WAIT FOR AN OPPORTUNITY,

BUT TO BE THE OPPORTUNITY,

AND BECOME THE OPPORTUNIST.

FREEDOM RIDER PLAYS WITH FIRE,

AND AS HIS UNDERSTANDING OF ITS FUNDAMENTAL VALUES

GROW HE BECOMES FLAME AND SPARK.

FLAME IN THE SENSE THAT HE WILL BURN.

AND SPARK AS IN BEING WHAT IS NECESSARY

TO SEE CHANGE IN HIS LIFETIME,

AND CHANGE IN HISTORY.

THE SOUND OF HIS HORSE

BEATING THE EARTH WITH EVERY HOOF MAKING A TRIUMPHANT SYMPHONY,

FOR THE HEARTS OF THE CAPTIVES KNOW WHEN THEY HEAR IT,

IT MEANS FREEDOM.

FREEDOM RIDER HAS BEEN CALLED HERE AND THERE,

BUT HE NEVER EXPECTED HE WOULD NEED TO LIBERATE

HIS OWN COUNTRY,

THE PLACE HE CALLS HOME,

FOR IT WAS BUILT ON FREEDOM,

ESTABLISHED TO FREE THE CAPTIVES.

BUT HE'S HARDLY HAD TIME

TO DEFEND THE HEARTS ACROSS OTHER NATIONS,

BOUND TO THE DUTY AND HEAVY RESPONSIBILITY

OF HIS OWN HOME.

YET HIS HEART WILL NEVER BE BROKEN,

HIS HOPE WILL NEVER DRY,

HIS EYES WILL NEVER PANIC,

AND HIS MIND WILL NEVER STRAY FAR FROM THE MISSION ON HAND.

THOUGH HE WILL NEVER GIVE UP,

HE KNOWS HE CAN'T DENT THE OPPRESSION ALONE.

ONE ANT IS ONLY SO MUCH IN THE FACE OF A BILLION.

HE NEEDS OUR HELP.

HE NEEDS OTHERS TO GATHER THEIR STRENGTH

AND RIDE AGAINST THE EASY PATH.

TO TAKE THE DIRTY MUDDY TRAIL,

AND MAKE SURE OTHERS STAY CLEAN.

TO STAND UP AGAINST WHAT EVERYONE ELSE
BELIEVES.

WILL YOU?

YOUR ANSWER MATTERS LITTLE TO FREEDOM
RIDER,

FOR HIS PURPOSE IS UNWAVERING.

PLUS HIS GATHERING HAS AT LEAST GROWN

FROM A PARTY TO ONE TO A PARTY OF TWO,

HE HAS BEEN JOINED BY ANOTHER.

EVEN THOUGH MORALLY THEY CHOOSE A DIFFERENT
PATH,

THE END GOAL IS THE SAME.

FREEDOM RIDER,

MEET THE MURDERER OF TRUTHS.

THE MURDERER OF TRUTHS

I DISSECT AND DEPICT EVERY TRUTH THAT CROSSES MY HEART.

EVERY SUBTLE LITTLE INSIGHT

INTO ANOTHER'S PHILOSOPHY

I EXAMINED WITH STEADY HANDS AND OPEN MIND.

AND I COME TO CONCLUDE

THAT MY PAST IS FILLED WITH ASSASSINS.

TAKING AND KILLING ALL THE SPACE IN MY HEAD,

CONQUERING EVERY INCH OF REAL ESTATE

I HAD LEFT TO THINK FOR MYSELF,

SUFFOCATING MY CAPABILITY

TO CREATE AND IMAGINE AND DEVELOP BELIEF.

YOU TOLD ME IT WAS FAIR!

YOU TOLD ME I COULD BE ANYTHING I WANTED TO.

WHAT IF I DIDN'T WANT TO BE RELIGIOUS.

WHAT IF I DON'T LIKE THE COLD FEELING OF SHACKLES AROUND MY ANKLES.

WHAT IF I HAVE BOLD NEW COLORS

AND I WANT TO SEE WHAT THEY CAN DO.

SO I CAUGHT AN ASSASSIN OFF GUARD,

AND TOOK BACK THAT SLICE OF PROPERTY.

I WILL FIGHT UNTIL MY MIND

IS RESTORED TO ITS RIGHTFUL CAPABILITY

TO LEARN AND MAKE JUDGMENT OF THE TRUTHS I PASS.

I AM A KILLER.

I WILL NOT REASON.

I WILL BELIEVE WHATEVER I FEEL IS RIGHT

AND THOSE WHO TRIED TO STOP ME

WILL FEEL MY BLADE PENETRATE THEIR SKULLS.

THEY WILL FEEL MY KNUCKLES

CRUNCHING THEIR BONES

AND SPLATTERING THEIR BRAINS

ONTO PLATTERS

WHERE I KEEP MY COLLECTION OF THE DEAD AT MIND.

I AM THE MURDERER OF TRUTHS.

YOU TELL ME THERE'S NO WAY.

THERE ARE SOME THINGS THAT ARE SIMPLY FACT.

YOU NEED TO GO TO COLLEGE,

WATCH ME NOT.

WATCH ME BUILD A LIFE MY OWN WAY,

AND WATCH ME BE HAPPY.

YOU'LL NEVER BE HAPPY BECAUSE YOU HOLD ONTO SO MANY THINGS,

SO MANY BELIEFS THAT YOU WILL ALWAYS HAVE OPPOSITION.

BECAUSE PEOPLE BELIEVE WHAT THEY CONCEIVE.

THEIR CONCEPTIONS

ARE FRAGMENTED MISDIRECTIONS

OF TRUE SATISFACTIONS.

AND THE ONLY TRUTHS YOU SHOULD HOLD ONTO

ARE THE ONES THAT LIVE IN YOUR HEART,

AND IS REMEMBERED IN YOUR BRAIN.

I HOLD TRUE,

THAT I AM ME,

AND THAT I CAN NEVER HAVE A DIFFERENT SOUL
NO MATTER HOW MUCH I WISH DIFFERENTLY.
I HOLD TRUE,
THAT I AM NOT SOMEONE
WHO CAN BLEND INTO A CROWD OF GRAY BLACK
AND WHITE
FOR I REPRESENT COLOR AND TASTE IN LIFE.
I HOLD TRUE,
THAT NO MATTER HOW HARD YOU COME AT ME.
NO MATTER WHAT TRUTH YOU HOLSTER IN YOUR
GUN,
I WILL STRIKE YOU DOWN
WITH GLORIOUS SWORDS OF SILVER AND GOLD.
I WILL MURDER EVERY TRUTH YOU SHOOT AT MY
HEART,
I AM BRICK AND MORTAR,
AND YOUR TRUTHS REPRESENT HOW IGNORANT
YOUR HEART IS.
AND LASTLY,
I HOLD TRUE THAT MY TRUTHS CAN NOT CHANGE.
MY OPINIONS,
MY STATEMENTS,
AND MY FEELINGS ARE ALL SUSCEPTIBLE
TO IMMENSE AND IMMEDIATE CHANGE,
BUT THEY WILL NOT BE GLUE.
THE ONLY THING THAT GETS MOLDED TO MY HEART
ARE THE TRUTHS THAT KEEP ME SANE,
SO WHAT HAVE YOU STUCK TO?
WHAT TRUTHS CAN YOU LET GO OF?
WE ALL HAVE THEM,

AND YOU BETTER HIDE.

MY BLADE IS GOOD AT FINDING

WHAT YOU DON'T NEED

AND SLAUGHTERING IT FROM YOUR CHEST.

THE ONLY TRUTH YOU SHOULD CARE ABOUT RIGHT NOW,

IS THE MURDERER OF TRUTHS STANDING ON YOUR DOORSTEP.

SONGBIRD

TWEET TWEET TWEET.

THAT'S RIGHT I'M A SONGBIRD MOTHERFUCKER.

AND I DON'T GIVE A DAMN WHETHER YOU WANT TO HEAR MY SONG OR NOT,

I'M GOING TO SING IT SO LOUDLY

YOUR BRAIN WILL CREATE CAVES

THAT ECHO MY NAME EVERY DAY ON REPEAT.

FOR MY SONG IS PURE.

AND IT'S BEAUTIFUL TO ME

IF YOU DISAGREE YOU CAN SHUT YOUR WINDOWS.

MY SONG IS NATURE,

MY SONG IS A CRY FOR JOY

SINGING OF HOW LOVELY IT IS TO FLY.

HOW LOVELY MY FEATHERS FRAIL IN THE WIND,

HOW PEACEFULLY I GLIDE.

I AM THE KING OF TREES AND THE KILLER OF BEES,

IF YOU MESS WITH ME I'LL PECK YOUR EYES OUT BITCH.

DON'T TOUCH ME,

I LIVE IN MY OWN PARADISE

YOU ENTERING THAT REALM

IS A DANGEROUS BOOBY TRAPPED MAZE

THAT'LL TAKE AND BREAK EVERYTHING YOU'VE KNOWN.

DON'T CHASE ME,

YOU'LL NEVER GET CLOSE ENOUGH TO UNDERSTAND

HOW I MOVE AND WHERE I'LL GO.

AND WHEN I FLY

YOU WILL HAVE NOTHING TO DO BUT WATCH.

AND I'LL CIRCLE AROUND

TO TAKE A VICTORY LAP IN YOUR FACE

FOR I HAVE WON

AND YOU KNOW YOU'LL NEVER DEFEAT ME AND MY
JOY.

SO BRING SOME GUNS IT'S YOUR BEST HOPE.

BUT WHEN I DIE,

THE SONGS OF MY KIND

WILL CARRY MY SOUL TO A PLACE

THAT YOUR COMMON AND UNSETTLINGLY DULL MIND

WOULD NEVER EVEN BE ABLE TO DREAM OF.

EXCUSE MY LITTLE BIRD SYNDROME.

I'LL GO BACK TO SINGING. TWEET TWEET TWEET.
FUCKER. TWEET TWEET TWEET.

SNOWSHINER ROUGHRIDER

SNOWSHINER AND ROUGHRIDER

WERE TWO PEAS OF THE SAME POD,

ONE FOCUSED ON PATIENCE

THE OTHER THREW HIS FISTS AND FOUGHT,

THOUGH SNOWSHINER KEPT THE SNOW PURE,

ROUGHRIDER SHOVELED TILL IT ALL DISAPPEARED

"WHERE IS THE SNOW ?"

SNOWSHINER CHOKED,

"DON'T YOU KNOW ?"

ROUGHRIDER BOASTS HIS COLLECTION OF BINS
FILLED WITH SNOW

SNOWSHINER BREATHED

BUT NOT IN RELIEF,

OH ROUGHRIDER BRINGS SUCH UNDENIABLE GRIEF

A SCOFF AND A LAUGH FROM ROUGHRIDER

PUSHED SNOWSHINER TO A POINT PAST

ANYTHING WE'VE EVER SEEN BEFORE.

SNOWSHINER LUNGED AT THE UNSUSPECTING
ROUGHRIDER

PINNING HIM TO THE GROUND.

HE RAINED PUNCHES FROM THE HEAVENS

UNTIL ROUGHRIDER BLED FROM HIS FOREHEAD,

'NEVER PUSH A GENTLE HEART.'

SNOWSHINER TOOK THE BINS

AND ONE BY ONE

RELEASED THEM BACK INTO THE FRONT YARD,

AND CLEANED EVERYTHING THAT WAS DONE UNTO
HIM.

ROUGHRIDER NEVER MESSED WITH HIM,

OR HIS WORK,

AGAIN.

MUSCLE MAN

THE LAST OF THE PEACEKEEPERS TO EXIT THE SHIP.

SMOKE FILLING THE DOORWAY

MAKING HIS ENTRANCE MORE DRAMATIC,

INTENSITY BUILDS AS WE WAIT TO SEE OUR HERO,

OUR BELOVED MUSCLE MAN.

IMAGES FLASH ACROSS PEOPLE'S MINDS,

A MAN WITH BICEPS THAT COMPARE WITH MOUNTAINS,

A TORSO MORE BUILT THAN A BUILDING.

CLEAN SHAVEN AND HANDSOME AS THEY COME,

IF HE LEADS EVERYONE WE HAVE HEARD OF SO FAR,

HE MUST BE SOMETHING TRULY EXTRAORDINARY.

OUT OF THE SMOKE EMERGES A MAN.

WOMEN AND YOUNG GIRLS ALIKE

GATHER BY THE ENTRANCE

IN DESPERATE ATTEMPT TO CATCH A GLANCE AT THEIR HERO.

BUT AS HE FILLS OUT OF THE SMOKE,

THERE IS A MINIATURE MAN,

MORE LIKE A KID.

THE CROWD IS CONFUSED,

HE MUST BE AN ASSISTANT.

HE STANDS 5'10

AND HIS SKIN AND BONE BUILD IS NOT ONE OF A HERO,

OR A LEADER.

HIS FACE COVERED WITH AN ALIEN LIFE FORM,

CALLED ACNE.

HIS HAIR NASTY AND CURLY,

HE WEARS A CAPTAIN AMERICA T SHIRT

AND BLACK SKINNY JEANS WITH A CUT AT THE KNEES.

HE FILLS INTO THE SIDE,

SONG BIRD RESTS ON HIS SHOULDER.

"WHAT WERE YOU EXPECTING?"

MUSCLE MAN SPITS.

"I AM THE MUSCLE MAN.

YOUR HEROES HAVE LITTLE STRENGTH,

THEIR LARGE MUSCULAR COMPLEXITY

BOASTS AN IMPRESSIVE INTERIOR,

ONE THEY WOULDN'T WASTE ON ANOTHER HUMAN BEING."

HE SPOKE IN A VOICE WARRANTING CHALLENGE,

IN FACT HE WAS INVITING.

BROAD SHOULDERED AND FULLY MASSIVE,

A LUMBERJACK

STANDING SIX AND HALF FEET TALL

STOOD LOOKING DOWN AT LITTLE MUSCLE MAN.

"YOU ARE PUNY. AND A DISGRACE TO MEN."

HE RAISED HIS AXE TO KILL

BUT WITH A ROLL BETWEEN THE LEGS OF THE LUMBERJACK,

MUSCLE MAN JUMPED ON THE MANS BACK

AND STABBED A KNIFE INTO HIS NECK,

CUTTING OFF HIS NERVOUS SYSTEM

AND CIRCULATORY VALVES ALL IN ONE FLUENT
MOTION,

HE JUST KILLED A MAN

IN TWO DIFFERENT WAYS SIMULTANEOUSLY.

THE CROWD ROARS IN APPLAUSE,

WHAT A SHOW.

"POWER EXISTS IN MANY FORMS.

THE TWO MOST IMPORTANT MUSCLES

ARE MY STRONGEST NO MAN OR ENTITY CAN TOUCH
ME,

WHY SHOULD PHYSICALLY STRONG PEOPLE

BE THE ONLY ONES WHO HAVE FUN.

I AM NOT A BARN BURNING FIRE AS THEY ARE,

I AM THE WATER.

I WILL BOIL AND STEAM

BUT IT IS MY ENEMY THAT WILL BE
EXTINGUISHED.

SO TRY ME.

BRING GUNS, BRING TANKS, AND JETS.

I'LL BRING HEART AND BRAIN,

THE ONLY TWO WEAPONS YOU ACTUALLY NEED.

MR. OPPRESSIONIST

BRING FORTH YOUR PEACEKEEPERS,

BRING AN ARMY, I WILL NEVER DIE.

CUT ME OPEN FROM THE OUTSIDE

AND YOU'LL FIND TEN LAYERS UNDERNEATH

WAITING TO BE UNCOVERED,

READY TO FLY.

THE SONGBIRD MAY SING A PRETTY TUNE,

BUT HE IS NOTHING WITHOUT HIS VOICE.

FREEDOM RIDER HAS DONE WELL FOR HIMSELF,

BUT A DEAD HORSE TURNS HIM INTO A WALKER,

AND WALKING WON'T REACH THE HEART OF THE MASSES.

A MURDERER, HE WALKS THE EDGE OF SANITY,

HE SEARCHES FOR THE ABSTRACT

BUT HE'S NOTHING WHEN I ABUSE HIM PHYSICALLY.

SNOWSHINER IS NOTHING

WHEN I INTRODUCE HIM TO SUMMERS HEAT,

I'LL MELT HIM TO A PUDDLE.

AND YOUR MIGHTY MUSCLE MAN,

HOW COULD I FORGET.

PERHAPS BECAUSE HE'S SO PUNY,

HEART AND MIND ARE POWERFUL ENOUGH

TO BEAT BRAWN BUT THEY'LL NEVER OVERCOME DISEASES.

I AM MR. OPPRESSION,

AND I LOOK TO PRESS ONTO THE CHESTS

OF EVERY MAN AND WOMEN

WHO DARE RAISE A FINGER TO THE SYSTEM.

ANYONE WHO CHALLENGES THE GATEKEEPERS,

SHALL FEEL THE WORK OF THE OPPRESSIONIST IN YOUR BONES.

I WILL WORK LIKE A SLOW MOVING MACHINE

SLOWLY TAKING OVER ALL THAT IS IMPORTANT TO YOU,

IF MY WORK IS DONE CORRECTLY,

YOU WILL NEVER NOTICE I EXISTED,

EVEN THOUGH YOU ARE MISERABLE AND ROTTING.

YOUR PEACEKEEPERS ARE MATERIAL FORM,

ANYTHING THAT TAKES ON A PHYSICAL PERSONANCE

CAN BE CORRUPTED.

WORDS, BIRDS, AND YES PEACEKEEPERS ARE NOT SAFE FROM ME.

TELL YOUR PHONY WEAK HEROES TO MEET ME IN THEIR MINDS,

THEY WILL FALL LIKE FLIES.

AND WHEN I'M THROUGH WITH THEM I'M COMING FOR YOU.

ENJOY FREEDOM WHILE IT LASTS.

FINAL SHOWDOWN

IN ORDER TO SUCCEED AGAINST OPPRESSION,

ONE SHOULD GATHER AROUND THOSE

HE OR SHE TRUSTS IN ORDER TO REMIND
THEMSELVES OF THE END GOAL,

AND KEEP THEIR EYES FIXED

ON THE CURVING PATH IN FRONT OF THEM.

WITHOUT A FRIEND YOU WILL TEETER TOTTER

ON YOUR PATH UNTIL YOU LOSE YOUR WAY
COMPLETELY.

I WISH I COULD TELL YOU OUR HEROES COME OUT
VICTORIOUS,

BUT AS I'M SURE YOU'VE NOTICED,

OPPRESSION STILL LIVES AND HE WORKS
STEADILY.

SONGBIRD LOST HIS VOICE,

BUT NOT BEFORE HE SHARED IT

WITH BILLIONS OF BIRDS AROUND THE WORLD,

WHO CARRY HIS SONG EVERYWHERE THEY GO.

MUSCLE MAN WAS BROKEN FROM HEAD TO TOE

BUT HIS STORY INSPIRED MANY

WHO WERE NOT AS PHYSICALLY STRONG AS
OTHERS.

FREEDOM RIDER INSPIRED THOSE FEW,

LIKE MYSELF,

TO TAKE UP THE PEN AND BECOME FREEDOM
WRITERS.

THE MURDERER OF TRUTHS TOOK THE BLOWS

UNTIL THE LAST TRUTH WAS BEATEN OUT OF HIS BRAIN,

NEVER TO KILL AGAIN.

BUT HIS WORK WAS PROOF

THAT NOT EVERYTHING SHOULD BE BELIEVED SO READILY,

BUT RATHER SHOULD BE PONDERED AND INVESTIGATED PERSONALLY.

SNOWSHINER WAS DELIVERED TO A PLACE

WHERE SNOW MELTS BY THE TIME IT REACHES SOIL,

HE COULD DO NO WORK ANYMORE.

BUT WHERE THE SNOW FELL

HIS FOLLOWERS WILL CLEAN THE SNOW FOR HIM.

WE MAY HAVE LOST THE PEACEKEEPERS,

BUT THEIR WORK IS INSPIRATION

TO SO MANY TO TAKE UP THEIR HARD WORK,

AND MAKE SURE NONE OF IT GOES TO WASTE.

OPPRESSION MAY LIVE,

AND HE DOES GREAT WORK,

BUT WE ARE COMING FOR HIM.

WE'RE COMING FOR THE GATEKEEPERS

THAT LOCK US OUT OF OUR INHERITANCE,

TO THINK FREELY, TO FEEL GLORIOUS,

TO BECOME SACRED.

WE ARE ALL WALKING PEASANTS UNTIL WE FIND CROWNS,

AND WE ALL HAVE ONE HIDING SOMEWHERE IN FRONT OF OUR EYES.

THE DAYS OF OLD YOU WERE BORN INTO ROYALTY,

BUT NOW ROYALTY IS ACHIEVED.

WE ARE THE NEXT GENERATION,

WE SEEK CHANGE, WE SEEK FREEDOM FROM OPPRESSION.

AND WE SEEK TO ENTER THROUGH THE GATES GUARDED BY THE GATEKEEPERS.

WE ARE THE DREAMERS,

AND WE ONLY GROW BIGGER,

JOIN US FRIEND

IT'S NEVER TOO LATE TO MAKE A DIFFERENCE.

SEASONS

summer

when summer dances with the seasons

its step is vigorous,

she is light on her feet.

she moves to an upbeat tune

and she loves the beach,

her colors of pink florescent sunsets

and endless blue sky reminds us

that she is our break from the cold.

her warmth rests heavily on our souls as we sleep,

she whispers subtly this summer is for upgrades.

with school tackled and not to return for months

it's time that we inject new objectives.

it's time to get to work.

it's time to train.

it's time to sleep,

soul search,

party,

binge watch,

whatever it is that you do it's time you do it.

for she is waiting with heavy expectancy,

and so are you.

it's summer, beauty, drama, adventure.
live it however you do.
it's the
only
way.

fall

as the colors change so do our faces.
our hard work can now look back
and see the distance it's covered.
we haven't reached the peak of this
mountain yet,
but we have come far from where we started.
the past summer was filled
with radical adventures that will soon
reshape into inside jokes and fairytales.
it's time for school again
and it's face is as bitter to see as any,
but at least the weather becomes bearable.
at least we are one year closer to an end,
one semester at a time
breaking down our school barriers
like a sledgehammer to a brick wall.
we are soldiers and the war has started
again.
so we look back down the mountain,
changing out our summer uniform
for a fall outfit,
seeing just how far we've come,
and just how far we have to go.

winter

dear winter branches,
it's time to abandon fall fashion.
snow is here
white powder blankets the ground
giving it new meaning and visual.
we add our extra layers
we grab our shovels and gloves
and we set off on icy roads.
we huddle closely
conserving our warmth by a fireplace
fire dances on logs, smoke fogs the night
sky,
and we chase warmth like its our lifeline.
i have fallen in love with the snow
for i placed my secrets
in chests and the snow hides them for me
now until the seasons change,
i know what i hold closest
will be safe.
the storms rage
tornadoes blow the trees away
and my friends fly away in the wind
promising to return one day.
scarves are wrapped tightly
like the gifts under the tree,
snow shoes removed from the closest
after a whole year of hiding.

it is winter.
and it is good.

spring

spring,

following up winter is no easy task.

and preceding summer

means you go mostly forgotten.

i guess you and me are much alike,

spring.

we are nobody's favorite.

and we both change and impact our surroundings,

we just don't get the credit we deserve.

we work in the silence

when people don't watch us,

for we don't crave attention like summer or winter.

we seek progression,

and freedom where we can get it.

we would love for love

but the other seasons are much too busy

baking in their own beauty and popularity.

no matter,

we will continue our work,

in the silence, praying one day,

we   may   be   someone's   favorite.

LOVELY SIDE OF THINGS

inhale

there's no way back,

the sky over every city filled with fire.

and then it all went quiet.

i felt her hands on the side of my face,

her thumbs wiping away my tears.

i felt the heat from her body.

i heard the catch of her breath.

and when our lips finally came together,

the kiss was urgent.

our bodies hungry for the warmth of the other's chest.

i looked up at her, inhaled.

i couldn't tell if my heart was breaking,

or bursting open with joy.

i only knew i didn't want to pull away for a single second.

and it was only when we both gasped for a breath

that i realized her eyes were squeezed shut,

her lashes were wet.

she whispered hoarsely,

"i'm sorry."
i pulled her closer,
"it's going to be alright."
the world may have ended,
but love still lives.
and it may be the only thing left that can
save us.

entangled humans

what more can we give each
other than our humanity?
take hands and feel flesh against your own,
be aware of the heat
flowing through tangled veins
beneath flawed skin
and around brittle bones.
life ends too quickly to pursue the perfect
and if we do so,
we will miss the joy
of accepting magnificent messes,
each refined by a lifetime spent
chasing the impossible.
i am human.
and i love you.
that's all i will ever know for certain.

        i thank you
love.
sit on the edge of my bed once more,
your hair spilling over your shoulders
like an ethereal waterfall,
majestically looking back at me
with eyes sparkling with questions
that i'd be happy spending my life
answering.
it is most relieving
when someone sees the real you,
and falls in love with that person first.
never a need to hide your stripes,
or filter thoughts and words around such a
love,
it's pure and beautiful and so rare.
i have felt such a comfort
and i consider myself a lucky one.
i thank you for giving me that.

a week to love

there's seven days until billions

of zombies reach our doorstep.

we could run,

and we'd live an extra three or four days.

but we decide instead to stay,

if this is the end

i want to hold the hand of the girl i've always loved.

you slept the first night

and i couldn't bear to do anything

but hold your tired body in my arms with tender care,

as tears roll down my face.

the second night we stayed up late,

we watched old sitcoms and ate popcorn,

we laughed at what they thought

the end of the world would be like.

the third night was a quiet one,

it seemed like days were passing

much too quickly for our liking,

we held each other and you told me how much you loved me,

and i told you how much i needed you.

the fourth night we sang and drank until we danced,

and danced until we drank,

and drank until we passed out.

on the fifth night we watched captain america,

and cried wishing he was here to save us,

and we chuckled at the thought

of a zombified steve rogers holding his shield,

you drew a cartoon of how you thought it would look,

your artistic beauty was my favorite thing about you.

the sixth night we held on so tight,

we didn't eat, we didn't drink, we didn't move.

the sound of billions of feet marching

was shaking the earth and house.

i wrapped myself around her,

they would be here within hours

and i would make sure i would die before her,

i couldn't bear the thought,

of seeing her being taken from me.

she told me she was scared,

i told her i was too.

she fell asleep in my arms one last time,

i loved her enough.

i would give my heart to replace hers when she loses it.

on the seventh night,

our lips came together

as zombies dug their nails deep into my back,

i sealed my eyes shut.

we promised that the last thing

we see of each other wouldn't be terror,

that way for eternity we could remember the beautiful things.

i heard her scream and out of reaction,

i took a peak as she was pulled to the ground,

cuts all over her forehead,

blood running like rivers down her face.

her eyes screamed for help,

but were still shut.

her hands stretched out for another.

i reached, and it all went black.

our week for love was over,

and so was this life.

so was this world.

percentages

let it be known

99.99% of the world

is going to need affection at some point in
there life.

99.99% of people who were born

needed a mother so we all have needed
something.

roughly 75% of us are nothing better

than a walking zombie failing to be active,

preying on the minds of the weak.

the 24% left are mute,

and will not speak up for others or
themselves.

that leaves just 1% of people

who look at their personal lives

as a tool to unlock better understanding.

as a lighthouse ready to guide in a ship.

as the sole bearing source

of a symbiotic based plague that can infect
millions.

the 1%.

more than half of that tiny little
percentage

will never know that there are more people
like him,

more people like her,

out there.

and i stumbled upon you, so lovely, unique, and blue.

and we came together in a dark nights sky

and became fluorescent light sources

beaming like spotlights for all to see.

we became fireworks,

and fire is hard to smolder when it exists in the clouds.

people admire us, people fear us,

people may never understand what we're capable of

because what we do is unlike things

you are used to comprehending.

we invite new thoughts

and awkward scenarios with open arms

for they form words your eyes wouldn't normally pick up.

never leave me my firework,

for its so much harder to be a spotlight alone,

and a percentage of me will wither away.

<u>Dark Cold</u> <u>World</u>

A DYING PLEE

OUR BRAINS TEETER

ON THE BRINK OF SANITY MORE THAN WE KNOW OR ARE AWARE OF.

WE ARE CACKLE MINDED,

SYCOPHANTIC, STOOGES

TRYING TO PIECE TOGETHER AN UNSOLVABLE VAGUE PUZZLE.

AND PERHAPS THAT

IS WHEN WE ARE TAKEN ADVANTAGE OF THE MOST.

AS WE INCH HELPLESSLY CLOSER TO OUR PRECIPICE,

THE OPPRESSION OF OUR OBLIGATIONS

MOUNT TALLER THAN MOUNTAINS.

IT IS HOPELESS.

WE HAVE NO ONE TO BLAME BUT OURSELVES,

IF ALL YOU DID WAS OPEN YOUR EYES

YOU COULD FATHOM THE MURDEROUS TORTURE

WE HAVE CURSED TO THE LIVING AROUND US.

KILLED OFF ALL THE TUNA,

ALL THE TURTLES AND LIONS.

OBLITERATED THOSE WHO WERE NOT DEALT GOOD HANDS,

CONCUSSED THOSE WE DON'T AGREE WITH,

FORMING A SOCIETY BUILT ON EVERY MAN FOR HIMSELF,

SURVIVAL OF THE FITTEST,

TURNED AROUND AND CALLED IT CAPITALISM.

WE HAVE TAKEN SO MUCH

THAT THERE'S NOTHING LEFT TO TAKE FROM ANYMORE.

AND WHAT IS THE RESULT?

WE SAY WE ARE "BALANCED."

BECAUSE WE LIVE IN MIDDLE CLASS TO WEALTHY SUBURBAN HOMES.

BECAUSE WE HAVE TWO BILLION TONS

OF WASTE PER YEAR,

AND ARE FILLING OUR OCEANS WITH COMPOST.

WE HAVE TRASHED MOTHER EARTH AND LITTERED HER SOIL,

SPIT ON HER TREES WHILE YOU ARE AT IT.

AND WE WRITE IT OFF,

BECAUSE THE GOVERNMENT WILL HANDLE IT RIGHT?

WHO DO YOU THINK PUT YOU THIS CLOSE TO THE EDGE SWEETHEART.

IT'S AS PLAIN AND AS SIMPLE AS INK ON A PAGE.

THE WORLD IS DYING,

THE PEOPLE ARE DYING,

YOU WILL SOON BE DEAD OR LIVING IN SHIT.

IT'S UP TO YOU TO STOP IT FROM HAPPENING,

IT'S UP TO YOU. WAKE UP.

SILENCE

I OFTEN WONDERED AS A CHILD,

WHAT MAKES MY PARENTS SO UNHAPPY.

WHY WOULD THE PREPARATION OF A MEAL

EVER LEAD TO SLAMMING FISTS

AND THE BREAKING OF OBJECTS.

NOW AS I GROW UP I KNOW IT.

I SEE IT.

I FEEL IT.

IT'S THE SILENCE,

THE DEEP EVER SO UNMOVING SILENCE.

NOT A SONG STIRRING IN THE MIND.

THEY CANNOT HEAR SINATRA

AS HE SINGS BEAUTIFUL MELODY.

THEY PUSHED HIM OUT,

FOR IT WASN'T PROFESSIONAL.

PROFESSIONS   PUSHED   OUT   JOY   FROM   THE
PRIORITY SEAT.

LOUIS ARMSTRONG'S RUCKUS OF JAZZ

HAS NO BUSINESS IN THE MIND OF A BUSY
BUSINESSMAN,

NOR IS THERE SPACE

IN A WORKING MOTHERS SCHEDULED BRAIN.

NO SPACE ON A MONDAY TO DANCE.

TUESDAY HAS BEEN BOOKED 24 HOURS OF NOT
FUN.

WEDNESDAY THROUGH FRIDAY IS FILLED

WITH THE JOBS SHE HATES

AND THAT LEAVE LITTLE FOR ANYTHING ELSE.
WHEN JOY ISN'T THERE TO SING A TUNE
LIFE IS FRUSTRATING.
AND THAT'S WHEN YOU AGE.
DISNEYLAND BECOMES A PLACE FOR TODDLERS,
NOT FOR YOU.
CHICAGO IS A DANGEROUS CITY
NOT A CONCRETE JUNGLE TO EXPLORE AND LOVE.
MARVEL MOVIES BECOME SIMPLY NOISE.
YOUR MIND TOO BOGGED DOWN
TO NOTICE THAT THERE'S COLOR
CIRCULATING IN BETWEEN YOUR EYES.
SILENT INTOXICATED MINDS
HAVE BEEN TORTURED AND BEATEN
BY A SOCIETY CLAIMING THE LIVES
OF INNOCENT DREAMERS.
I CRY FOR THEM.
A MONOCHROME LIFE,
THEY HAVE CONVINCED THEMSELVES
IT'S ALL THEY'LL EVER NEED.
IT'S ALL BUT OVER,
IT'S A MIND THAT'S RUSTED
AND STOPPED LOOKING FOR BETTER.
THEY CAME TO A PLACE,
A DARK AND SINISTER KINGDOM, CONTENTMENT.
SO SORELY MISSING THE TARGET,
THEY HIT ANOTHER ONE THEY DIDN'T MEAN TO.
THEY WERE CLAIMED BY SOCIETY,
AND I SWEAR TO DO EVERYTHING I CAN

TO SAVE PEOPLE NOT FROM THEIR LIVES,
BUT FROM CONTENTMENT.
THERE'S ALWAYS SOMETHING TO CHASE,
WHETHER IT IS THE WILD YOU CRAVE DEEP DOWN,
OR IF THE BEST LIFE YOUR HEART FEELS
IS A HOUSE ON A BEACH FOR RETIREMENT.
YOU MUST NOT GIVE UP,
YOU CAN'T LET SOCIETY WIN.
YOU CAN'T LET MONEY BE THE DICTATOR.
YOU CAN'T LET CONTENTMENT OVER POWER.
AND NEVER,
LET YOUR HEART GO SILENT.

in response to my mentor

'these little town blues are melting away
i'm going to make a brand new start of it
in old new york
and, if i can make it there, i can make it
anywhere
new york new york'
we are empty cold hearted creatures
living in suburbia with
not an adventure within a hundred miles,
new york is so far away.
our vagabond shoes stuffed in a safe,
and guarded by the gatekeepers.
these gatekeepers built metropolis
and watchtowers for the dreamers,
but we cannot see.
our telescopes and binoculars
destroyed in fire by arson.
it's no joke,
the quiet neighborhood says so much.
not a siren, or a car horn,
not even the waving trees speak out here.
silence is a torture tactic to the sane
and considered inhumane for the insane
yet we build rows of houses
that speak of no creativity,
no imagination, no love.
chicago is love.

san francisco is creativity.

new york is breath into lungs.

but the suburbia offers nothing

except cheaper living.

humanity has followed the path of least resistance too long.

we want to be safe,

financially secure,

and away from the chaos.

but it's the chaos that reminds us

that we aren't as sophisticated as we think.

we are two-legged animals

with a complicated language and lifestyle.

we are not gods who rule this planet.

for if this is our kingdom

we are doing a terrible job,

destroying it without any regret.

primitive thoughts move mountain and stone,

it's the overthinkers

and these gatekeepers

that locked up our spirits

into a society we didn't ask to be a part of.

and i've learned enough from my mentor.

to rise above and say,

i'm tired of losing this battle.

so it's time,

i do it my way

'for what is a man

what has he got
if not himself
then he has not, to say the things
he truly feels
and not the words
of one who doesn't kneel
i took the blows and did it my way.'

STATISTICS

FACT, SUICIDE IS THE THIRD

LEADING CAUSE OF DEATH FOR PEOPLE 15-24.

SEA TURTLE POPULATIONS HAVE DROPPED 95%.

ONE IN FIVE WOMEN

ARE SEXUALLY ASSAULTED IN COLLEGE.

HALF OF OUR MARRIAGES FAIL.

HALF OF OUR FORESTS CUT DOWN.

AND WE SIT BY,

WE LET THE NEWS TELL US

THE STATISTICS WHILE WE KEEP LIVING OUR
LIVES

WITHOUT CHANGE.

BECAUSE AS DISASTROUS AS ALL THAT IS,

IT'S NOT ME RIGHT?

IT'S NOT ON YOU,

AT LEAST NOT YET.

IS IT NOT ON US AS WE WATCH

OUR PLANET SELF DESTRUCT

FROM INSIDE BRICK AND MORTAR?

IS IT NOT ON US,

WHEN OUR KIDS ARE STRESSED AND DEPRESSED

BECAUSE OUR EDUCATION TEACHES SUCH THINGS,

AND WE LET THEM?

IS IT NOT ON US WHEN WE GIVE UP

ON OUR SPOUSE AT THE FIRST BUMP IN THE
ROAD,

LIVING IN FEAR THAT

YOU'LL WASTE YOUR TIME WITH SOMEONE YOU DON'T TRULY LOVE.

WHEN OUR ANIMAL KINGDOM

RUNS OUT OF FORESTS, OR OCEANS,

OR WETLANDS AND MOUNTAINS,

AND WE MAKE INNOCENT BEASTS BECOME MEMORIES,

WHERE DOES THE BARREL OF THE GUN POINT.

THE BITTER TRUTH IS

HUMANS ARE MUCH BETTER AT FEELING BAD FOR THEMSELVES THAN THEY ARE AT MAKING A DIFFERENCE.

THERE IS SO MUCH TO FIX,

AND ALMOST EVERYONE WHO READS THIS,

LET ALONE IF THEY FEEL LIKE THEY SHOULD OR NOT,

WILL DO NOTHING TO STOP ANY OF THIS FROM HAPPENING.

BECAUSE YOU FIGURE SOMEONE WITH MORE POWER,

MORE OBLIGATION WILL FIX THIS.

BUT THAT LINE OF THOUGHT

WILL CONTINUE ON AND ON

UP THE HIERARCHY UNTIL

YOU REACH THE PEOPLE

WHO HAVE MADE THESE STATISTICS BECOME REALITY.

IT'S ON OUR SHOULDERS,

TO PLACE OURSELVES

INTO THE BATTLEFIELD DEAD CENTER AND NOT MOVE.

STAND FACE TO FACE WITH THE OPPRESSIONIST

AND SPIT ON HIS SHOE WHEN HE TELLS YOU TO
'SHOO'.

YOU'RE THE ONLY HOPE WE HAVE

TO SAVE OCEANS AND TEENAGERS,

FORESTS AND MARRIAGES, SEXUAL ASSAULT
VICTIMS,

AND THE MANY OTHER THINGS THAT NEED FIXING.

IT'S ON YOUR SHOULDERS,

AS AN INDIVIDUAL ENTITY.

SO DO NOT LOOK AROUND,

DO NOT LOOK UP, LOOK INWARD,

YOU KNOW WHAT YOU NEED TO DO.

WHAT NEEDS SAVING?

HOPE

cardboard castle

you've lost everything
no money, no contacts,
no job, no car
your soul is perishing
you have nothing left in your heart.
you walk the streets
carrying the face of defeat
and you see no meaning
to anything.
then you stumble upon a man,
a homeless man
says he fought back in iraq and iran
came home to a struggle far worse
than even the taliban.
yet he smiles,
it's a smile you haven't seen in a while
genuine sincere and not complex
it simply says, i'm happy.
and you stand there in disbelief.
wondering what exactly it takes to achieve,
and what achievement really means
perhaps everything is not as it seems.
perhaps a cardboard box,

is in truth a cardboard castle.

maybe everything else in life is an extra hassle.

when the true battle, is trying to be happy.

i am seventeen and i should have a lot to think about.

most people my age

sit and gossip and pout.

but i will choose happiness every single time

and to that there is no counter.

community

community abolishes the need to compare and to compete.

we all struggle

with feeling lesser than our peers sometimes,

but when we take the time

to know each other's stories,

we realize that we are all in this world together.

so why not celebrate each other?

what stops us from encouraging another?

there's room on this planet for all to succeed,

there's no reason

to have prizes for only one,

we will all win at something if we worked together.

can you make someone's day better?

without effort it's impossible to know.

give it a try at the least.

that's all i ask.

be love

believing is loving
so in order to be living you
must be loving.
but living is something
i haven't accomplished
and it reflects on my ability to love.
love life so that you can live,
but without love in my life,
living is embarrassing.
embarrassment is the key to sadness
and sadness is a long way from love
which puts me far from the living.
i'm a tree planted in a factory,
looking for the sun to give me energy s
o i can thrive.
but in order to thrive
you have to be felt,
by the suns rays.
feeling is thriving
being felt is being thrived.
but being felt requires me
to twist my trunk and bend my branches
into positions i've never been comfortable
before,
and people will see my efforts to do
something
which seems so simple

and they'll laugh at me.

being the butt end of a joke

is a long way from thriving.

it's as far as a bug trapped

in a car trying to find home.

you crawl to the window where you see the open world,

it's a place more familiar.

but you're stuck an surrounded

by people trying to kill you

and step on you and wipe you away

simply because you look different.

and you sound different.

you feel weird.

if only they understood you need those extra legs

to get to places two footed creatures shouldn't go.

if only they were patient enough

to realize you are harmless and mean no harm.

if the people of this world

would stop stepping on each other's faces

maybe then we would all be able to believe.

and then we could all love.

and thrive.

and be felt not just on our bodies but in our souls.

stop loving.

for that is an action and

actions are temporary.
but instead
become love.
for becoming is unstoppable.
be love.

THE OTHERS

*The Star the Failure the Success
You*

At the end of life

we will look back,

and we will reflect on our choices.

Maybe it will be a moment slow,

like syrup dripping from a nearly empty
bottle.

Or perhaps it will be quick like lightning,

nobody would know the answer to that.

Either way I believe

we will look past our successes and see our
mistakes.

Not in a painful, regret filled way,

but in almost a humorous light.

Seeing how hard we tried for vain,

for hopeless endeavors and lovers,

and for something so stupid as pride.

We caught the edges of puddles and fell
face flat,

we drove our bikes into trees.

We drove our cars into other cars.

We got bad grades sometimes,

and it was the end of the world at the
time.

And after all those memories,
we give ourselves the credit
of looking at those times
we pulled our face out of the puddle.
Yes, we failed English classes,
but we still became poets.
Sure we were broke
and didn't have money for fun,
but we still created the best backyard fun
with nothing at all.
And we let ourselves go completely.
We let go of our Peter Parker,
we said farewell to Steve Rogers
and became Captain America
and Spiderman.
What's the message?
Go for it.
Dream a bigger dream.
Live life every day
thinking   of   new   ways   that   you   can
gloriously fall
flat on your face.
Then perhaps our last few moments might put
a smile on our faces.
A smile that will last an eternity.

    Remembrances

"Do you remember Thomas?"
No, no I don't.
I remember a man,

he wore a blink-182 shirt

and black skinny jeans,

had curly brown hair

and blue eyes that said more than he intended.

he crossed his arms

to say don't look at my skinny nature,

he kept eye contact for all of two seconds.

But no who's Thomas?

"Do you remember Hannah ?"

Doesn't ring a bell.

I do remember a girl

who wouldn't be caught dead

in clothing that wasn't black.

Her colored hair

a testament that she played

by her own rules.

Her bright eyes and beautiful

smile were a reason she was a leader to so many,

but the way it quickly faded

was true of how few she would call friend.

Leader of the lonely,

ruler of her free spirit,

and stolen before her reign could see it's end.

That Hannah?

Names are not my forte.

But I can recall a face.

and eyes.

and hearts.

That burn so bright.

My memory works through a metaphysical lens,

I see deeper than the average mind would try to depict.

And it's my blessing and my curse,

my glory and downfall.

And I would trade nothing

to lose that side of me,

for it's how I can feel soul

and music in another's heart.

Dear Me in the Future,

I hope all is well.

I hope you're living in a converted van,

sleeping in a beach parking lot

watching a golden sunset send rays of happiness

deep into your sternum.

I hope you've learned to play the ukulele,

and I hope you strum your hearts notes with ease.

I wonder how many bracelets

you've sold from the back of your van,

I'm sure business is tough.

And how many dogs do you have?

I suspect three or four,

anything else would be upsetting.

Well I don't mean to take up too much of your time,

one thing that'll never change about us

is our need to just sit and think

about everything not dared to be thought of.

One last question though,

did you fall in love with her?

Does she know how you really felt,

the aching in your heart,

the pit of darkness and despair

reserved for failure in this instance.

the deep deep love, the tender care,

the willing to drop everything and run for
it.
if she doesn't,
I'm sure what's on your mind is regret,
I pray one day you'll get over it.
Perhaps there will be beauty in life
with a different face.
Remind yourself the sunset
is a production that you get the privilege
of watching.
Love your pups,
love the beach and we'll get through this.
Believe in yourself,
you see things differently.
We all do.
With care,
your past.

Everything I Didn't Say

I do regret the long silences.

The times my vocal cords refused to move.

I sat there not in blank

but filled with banks of words and phrases.

Phrases of how I want to be free of society,

how I think teenagers are unwise,

and schemes of being a kid forever.

I couldn't bring myself

to talk about them

for I knew how I would be received,

or rather misconceived,

as I knew that my words are things not often spoken.

And in a generation where

status quo is the lifeline to social satisfaction,

I knew rejection wasn't far away.

So I stayed silent when my heart longed to scream.

I kept my lips shut for I feared acceptance,

I feared being wrong about it all.

There is no greater fear

than finding exactly what you want.

Nothing so profound

as a human actually accomplishing their goal.

Because what's next?

When you find everything you want,

you are filled, and soon completely empty,

for you're no longer chasing,

you have caught.

You're no longer running the race,

you have won.

So if I found the person

who could sing my song and find my peace,

I would be, complete.

My race won in first place with a grand prize.

And what's left?

There is no answer until you have it,

and the fear,

the chance of finding nothing leaves me silent.

Afraid to say everything that I haven't.

Beautiful But Filtered

The ugly truth of it all

is that some of us were born

to see the world in a different way from most.

Colors and make believe worlds

jumping out of manholes,

running across streets,

and bouncing off walls

placing my brain into a state of mental warfare

trying to determine the reality from the fiction.

Often those who are placed in the folders

of weird or different feel left out from society,

we are the broken pieces

that can't fit into the puzzle.

Our disease,

this plague of visionary optical resolution,

no longer can be deceived as a gift.

the conflict is that those who don't see the colors,

or the imaginary worlds,

still see beautiful things.

beauty is different in all of our hearts

processed through different filters

and regulatory palpitations.

those who live ordinary lives

will still see beautiful things in their lives.

Even though these beautiful things

are only fragmented scrambled particles

of what is truly beautiful,

they are processed the same.

So I beg to ask you, who actually is to gain.

The man who has bought into the broken society,

lives with obscured vision

and is unaware of his condition,

seeing beautiful in things that are far from.

or the man who comprehends

and acknowledges the broken fall state of our society.

his optics relaying information

that average is awful,

and beauty is a lifelong chasing

that may never be won.

who's to profit.

Broken lives breaking to the broken system

designed to crunch the craniums of the wonder people.

For there's nothing more torturing

to live alone in a world

full of brainwashed people,

perfectly content to be content,

people chasing nothing at all.

Carry On

Outright,

filled with fright,

carry on through this damned night.

Torches and flame set blaze to my joy.

Then you dealt your wild cards till now

and there's nothing left

for you to deal with but me,

a worthy adversary,

you crossed paths with the wrong visionary,

the unslayable mercenary,

with no weapon greater than pinpoint vocabulary.

Outright,

filled with fright,

carry on through this damned night.

Your weapon of mass destruction and global catastrophe.

You chose the belligerence,

said the only pay now is resilience,

shot people down for their difference,

so damn fearful but I call it ignorance.

Outright,

filled with fright,

carry on through this damned night.

This proves quite an enigma.

For who am I to point a finger at a fingerless killer,

the ceremonial dance of gun and trigger,

my hand picks up pen, while yours is busy
on twitter,

what chance does your slang have on
something bigger,

more permanent, more meaningful, an emitter

you call yourself a trickster while I am
the gravedigger.

We are not parallel.

For one of us lives in the most important
house

in the country while the other does not.

A big white house,

with so little to display.

So this is for us the people,

outright,

filled with fright,

please,

carry on through this good night.

Deeply Poetic

It's something you feel deep in your bones.
An outpouring for a good thing
that is self sustained
by your capability to be you.
It's a refresher that you behold
colors that can only be worn by you,
for you, inside of you.
When you find that good thing,
and it helps you forget
about all that you've done wrong,
instills hope and reinstalls clarity.
You remember you have purpose
and a life by which you control
how that purpose drawn energy is used.
Poetry is how I strip down my clothes
and view my nakedness,
my impetuous imperfection that I call my mind.
It's how I seek out my star in the sky,
I know one day that place
will have poetically scripted lines
dotting its infrastructure.
Empowering your soul is essential to finding peace,
find what draws you far away from reason.
A place where you roam in the wetlands free,

dancing on a beach

in the middle of the rainforest,

and your worries are stuck

high above the clouds only to reach you

through a precipitation that kisses your cheeks

and you laugh,

you dance, you thrive,

rain makes you stronger.

Your fire is fueled by your love.

Your good thing is powered and solar,

waiting to be turned on,

to be used.

Never stop chasing, doing,

believing in your good thing.

For I am inside my dreams in my writings and I will not be denied what I deserve, neither should you.

Poems Minus The Length

    i.

CUDDLE ME

    ii.

never have i ever,
and no i don't mean the game created
for teenagers to brag upon
sexual slash unlawful experiences.
never have i ever,
and no i am not about to tell
a long sophisticated lie,
as you would to a superior
like a boss or such,
to avoid some deep shit
that'd bite me in the ass
when i ask for that raise.
"no i would never ever mix drugs
into larry's soda boss."
no.
no never, not in a hundred million
gazillion years,
have i ever seen such a thing as you.

and all i can ask is

what star do you call yours ?

some say we are stardust,

fallen from the heavens like grains of sand,

so i wonder perhaps

i dream that those we are closest to

are part of the same star.

thanks for sharing the dust cap,

never stop shining,

never stop glowing,

for you give the night sky

an illumination only the most oblivious will overlook.

you make the solar system i reside in

more colorful and easier to navigate,

how could i ever

thank you enough.

iii.

You are the missing star

from the night sky

that came to earth

in search of a partner

to dance with.

iv.
i yell at the top of my lungs,
i frolic in fields, i have a good life.
i am a dog, but i
can still teach you
a thing or two about joy.

        v.
i swear, no i vow, no.
i promise, that i will never
fall in love with you.
my swears and vows
have failed me before though this,
promise, cannot be broken.

        vi.
from the treetops
we could see the future
of humanity's
fallen state.

        vii.
from the cliffside
we could see the sun's rays
burn holes in our frowns

and as it set,
we began to rise.

     viii.
from the ashes
our failures
were extremely visible,
we burnt every page left
in the book of us.

ix.
drop your shackles
rip off the uniform of uniformity
we escape tonight
in the name of distinction.

     x.
even the singing idri
knows your songs by heart,
and sings your tune
till his heart is all but content.

     xi.
an ocean rages
with the power of hundreds
of nuclear bombs
yet no politicians see her as a threat.

xii.
a descending ascension
sending us to a place
that may finally be the answers
to our problems,
balance.

xiii.
i cannot see through you,
for you are fog
you only let me see
as much of you
as you care to show.

xiv.
your placement in my life
has eclipsed even the light of the sun
though i am still blinded by your touch.
by your love.

xv.
to be dining with the kings
that are also thieves
in a room of gold and a filled treasury.

oh, its the pirate life for me.

        xvi.
wine never meant to hurt someone
but her relationship with poison
was the death of so many mouths.

        xvii.
though i am changed,
not for good or better
i am new
and i am a trendsetter.

        xviii.
the space between
two grains of dust
is being slowly separated by time
a natural disaster.

        xix.
we wait patiently
we wait for so long
for our dreams to become a reality,
and without a little work
we will wait eternity.

        xx.
the truth is
that our failings will never

take the place of our youthful romance,
you trip we dance
you sing we play
we dream you envision,
i pray that i live in the vision as well.

xxi.
how backwards is humanity
when we've created methods to madness
but no method to peace or happiness.

    xxii.
quit pretending like you
own the lot sweetheart
has nobody told you
soft spots are reserved
for the grateful?

xxiii.
peace is when the world
is ending and all you have left
are the things you love most.

xxiv.

ask yourself the question

are you better

than the you in the other dimension?

xxv.

for in the face of a bold enemy

i am their widowmaker

grim reaper

i am their slayer.

xxvi.

those that walk with you

on your path

will decide which path

you walk on next

the path of destiny.

xxvii.

i would never accept violence

as the solution to a problem

but everyone needs to be pushed at some
point.

xxviii.

for as a farmer places stakes

to support the weight

of heavy branches so it can grow and
produce fruit
i will carry your heaviness
so you can flourish
into everything you want to be.

xxix.
when our biggest fears
become places with no service
humanity becomes entirely
evident and entirely worthless.

xxx.
there are only two things
that can never die
love
and nature.

PROSE
an a.c. series

june 16, 2016//6:55pm
if only for a moment,
i could forget what
your lips taste like.
if only that moment
could last for a lifetime

june 27,2016//9:36pm
let the souls
intertwine
and let yourself
get lost
in something
you've never experienced

july 5, 2016//5:44pm
you know what i want?
i want to feel the
grace of your soul
on mine. i want
to be the one you go to
at 3am when you can't

sleep. to feel you like no
one else has. to invade
your body like the
smoke from your
cigarettes. to know your body like
i know the lines of your face. i
want to feel you like
the rain on my fingertips.
i want to be consumed
in your beauty and poise.
and i just
want you to know me like i want
to know you.

july 13, 2016//1:40pm
he is green
like the specks in his
eyes.
blue like the thoughts
circling his head.
red like the fire
in his veins.
he is the onslaught
of color after a
rainstorm.
he is all the colors mixed together; a
special formula that
only he can concoct.

the world is grey.
but he is the color.
the color that brings me home

august 2, 2016//11:12pm
my muse is lost.
lost among seas of faces
and the sounds of shrill utterances.
voices on top of voices.
lost among cheap cologne
and the faint aroma of stale cigarette
smoke.
lost in the pages of a journal
i'll never get to indulge in.
lost in melancholy pain that is seldom
spoken of.
with no trace, it has left.
and there is a qualm that
it may never return

august 21, 2016//10:30pm
don't you get it?
it's you.
it's always been you.
but it'll never be me.

august 22, 2016//10:44pm
ONE DAY I'LL MOVE ON.
BUT I DON'T KNOW

IF I WANT TO.

october 2, 2016//8:04pm
there are endless clouds
and an endless sky.
so much space and
nothing to occupy it.
but it's better that way.
everyone else is aboard a flight

i'm chasing the sun

october 23, 2016//6:39am
dawn breaks on a new day,
but i still think of you

december 15, 2016//10:08pm
in the glow of the street lamp,
i see nothing but drops of rain
falling; falling hard.
falling harder
than i did for you

december 30, 2016//8:35pm
i see the sun,
finally
with all its other
stars

february 4, 2017//7:27pm
let me photograph you
right here
right now.
so i'll remember
the way you looked
and the way you exuded love
when you forget me

april 17, 2017//6:33pm
his eyes challenge me
but it never feels like a threat…
the light from the windows is casting
a glow upon his already shining
personality, making him radiate the
warmest light i've ever known.
wonder; excitement, they fill me.
all the way to the top.
he is home; the ever-glowing
light that guides

april 22, 2017//11:32pm

if i told you the color of his eyes
you wouldn't believe me.
and i don't say that to doubt
your gullibility…
i say that because the colors are
unbelievably contrasting
and complicated
and complimentary
all at the same time.
a riddle i don't think i'll ever solve.
never in a million years…
but if that mean i'd spend the million
years looking into them
that would be everything i'd ever need.

may 11, 2017//4:55pm
i watched a rose die,
outside my window.
every day, i always said,
"i should water that".
but i never did.
and now it's dead.
because of me.

may 16, 2017//4:17pm
when you touch me
i feel it;
a thousand suns
melting into my skin,
warming me to my core.
i feel it; warmth.

june 13, 2017//12:00am
maybe i'm tired
of just friends.

june 20, 2017//11:39pm
i took a chance
and got stuck
and i tried and tried
but you wouldn't let me go

july 17, 2017//10:18pm
i want to write about you
until my hand is numb
i want to feel you
i want, i want, i want,
but all you do is take.
until there's nothing left;
not even a beat in my heart.

august 4, 2017//8:23pm

i am infatuated with
(the thought of)you.

i think of you
every now and again
what we could be and who we could be
but i know you never think of me

august 4, 2017//8:27pm
at a moment's glance
i see you and me.
but then, a glance
only lasts a moment

august 21, 2017//9:52pm
you were like an overexposed polaroid.
i waited
and waited
and waited some more,
but it turns out i was just waiting for
nothing.

october 2, 2017//6:12
i want to step into
an abyss
because if there's nothing there
maybe i'll find myself.

october 10, 2017//1:01pm
how do you fight war?
love.
but what if there isn't anymore to give?

october 29, 2017//4:57pm
in flight-
suddenly we were enveloped
in clouds

senseless, no recognition of direction

dark, stormy… grey took over

we disappeared

we had a secret from the world

november 14, 2017//5:39pm
she may not realize now
but when she does
oh boy
when she does,
there will be a storm
a great storm

november 16, 2017//8:10am
one turned to four
bikes turned to automobiles
we grew up
but you still make me feel the same

december 3, 2017//6:25pm
more star-crossed than soulmates

december 10, 2017//10:54pm
is it your walls
or mine
that could tell more about us

january 3, 2018//6:14pm
dear mr. serotonin,
i like it when you're around.

january 18, 2018//4:27pm
the ominous sky threatens most

but not me

i am one with the clouds

january 23, 2018//3:28pm
i'm not a religious person in the least
but i pray you see the mistakes you've made

january 23, 2018//7:58pm
there is an overabundance
of so many things in this world

but never time.

february 7, 2018//6:08pm
the creamsicle sky
calls me home

february 9, 2018//4:30pm
i'm so good at imagining

pretending.

why am i like that?

my prose exists as
a child of an idle life
but a mind bursting
with prismatic colors

i can turn a dying light
into a beautiful flame

and ignite dreams
of someone i seldom know
about or of

someone who doesn't know me

i'm someone who longs to know them

i am the steady boat
asail on the seas; constant

never changing

but maybe i should.

march 14, 2018//6:24pm
NEVER AGAIN.

march 14, 2018//6:25pm
the timing was off

it's not your fault

it's not your fault

but it's not mine either.

march 15, 2018//8:11am
your arms are a jail

and i will not be held prisoner
any longer.

march 15, 2018//1:42pm
what is most desirable?

a mutual understanding between two,
when it doesn't turn out
quite right.

like annie and walter atop the plaza

i need you to understand where
i'm coming from.

because trust me,
i understand where you're coming from

it's what got us here
in the first place.

march 20, 2018//2:46pm
if i could paint you a picture

as blue and as meaningful
as this morning

you'd be in a bliss
like no other

you'd understand

march 20, 2018//4:11pm
i sometimes remember it;

the weight of your hands on mine

the graceful touch of your love

taken away faster than the speed
of light

let's go back

you and i

back to the good times

when the pressure of your love
didn't suffocate me

march 22, 2018//12:57pm
on rainy days
i feel like everything is going
to be okay

march 25, 2018//5:02pm
if rubber bands weren't meant
to be stretched
do you think people would have made them?

march 27, 2018//11:26pm
you won't die, trust me

i've already immortalized you
with my pen

april 1, 2018//7:08pm
you make me question so many things

including myself

and i have yet to recognize if
that is good or bad

AND FINALLY

wonder

we will never know where we go when we die.

we will never feel love until we've felt love.

we will never experience serenity

until we enter a place that is serene.

world peace, as we know,

is something hipsters chase with vigorous passion,

it would be rare to have a conversation with one

and not hear it come up in some manner.

it's a goal we can all support,

but some of us would see it as impossible,

someone will always be upset with someone.

metropolis is known as a home

to a large sum of people in a closely knit area

magnified by lights encroaching on the night sky

giving it tint.

hiding the lives of stars,

and, the view of the stars.

everyone has an opinion of city,

it's busy, it's crazy,

it's scary.

it's beautiful, it's atmospheric,

it's a keystone of creativity.

fears.

everyone has them,

everyone actively avoids intercourse with
intimidating things.

so you fear the city,

you fear the forest,

you fear public transportation.

you fear fire,

you fear water,

you fear eight legged creatures the size of
your fingernail.

you fear love,

some of us even fear accomplishing

everything we've ever wanted to do.

fear has an antonym,

and i'm not talking about bravery.

i do not speak of the word courage.

the word is wonder.

wonder and fear cannot operate together.

they will clash heads

like that of roman gladiators or spartans.

that of republicans and democrats.

that of fire and of water.

wonder works in ways

which envelope your heart

and package your heart to be sent off to a
new place.

fear fears movement.
fear feels foreign influence
and reminds you not to move too far.
to stay away from new,
to eat away at itchy feet.
wonder draws attention
to the things you are not familiar with
and asks you to try.
for it's our duty to do what pleases us.
to do what breathes life back into us.
to do what puts life into our bloodstream
entering our fingertips and
electrocuting purpose into our atmosphere.
wonder says be fucking crazy to those that
don't move
out of the inner circle of normality.
to run through san francisco
proclaiming yourself a god to the hundreds,
to the masses who walk beside you.
your victory urging you to diminish fear.
we all have fears of varying difficulties.
some may never be defeated,
some have stone ceilings
and you are merely a kite.
but as impossible as the view appears,
we are called
to call out stone and
bring hammer and tank.
for all walls are meant for breaking,

all roofs are meant for shaking,

every fear is yours for the taking.

i wonder what a world without fear

would look like.

perhaps a world a hipster would be proud
of.

perhaps a world of purpose

and beauty

and star gazing.

perhaps a world kind of complicated but
fully perceptive and full of intuition.

your homework is to wonder,

wonder inside of you.

wonder what you could feel that causes
urges in your stomach,

wonder what holds you

from promised gold,

wonder where to next.

awe

if you've ever laid on your back
and gazed on a night sky
a sky filled with thousands
upon thousands of stars
that say a thousand more words than...
i'm sorry, i couldn't finish that
i promised myself
that in a poem of awe-inspiring feeling
that i wouldn't mention things
that are anything but extraordinary.
so feel free to fill in the blank
with whatever feeling
you feel is fulfilling.
but mind the gap
that pulls you to the depths
and draws your focus
far from what was the start.
never wander far
for this is not the tale of wonder
this is awe.
this is not about the thunder
it's all raw emotion.
if you've ever done something
and lived it to the full
and right in the thick of the woods
you look over to see a golden sunset
as it dodges between trees

warming your cheeks on a cold

snowy morning you know what i'm talking
about.

pet owners hold testament

when your dog hurts his paw

and he limps straight to you

because he knows your hand by heart

it not only feeds

it provides

it's a source

to all necessary requirements for
happiness.

people who have played sports

know the road to accomplishment

is filled with very few

awe-inspiring moments

for hard work bears a brutal face

like a brick wall fastens

in front of a sledgehammer.

but you know, when the clock ticks to zero

your team's got the most goals

most points, most wins

and you lift up a trophy

with reckless abandon

for you accomplished the very thing

you never thought.

even people who have done the very simple

you made something cool

and people appreciated it

and you feel so accomplished.
in this world
the awe-inspiring moment is hard to come
by.
with the business
that we let fill our lives
and eat away at our free time
we diminish awe and we replace it
with stability.
but we aren't supposed to live life safely.
we aren't supposed
to be afraid of dying
or falling, or running.
for it's in those moments
when everything goes wrong
and you get low
that you look through
and see something so simple
as a vibrant plant
or a squirrel eating an acorn
a hummingbird as it hovers
a homeless man that smiles
a wild human on a mission
eyes that say ten thousands words
and three different emotions.
you look back and realize
you fell asleep on a plane
that soared above clouds themselves
you took the train

but didn't pay attention
to where it was going
you took a whale watching boat ride
and never took your phone
out of your hands
for this was no vacation
this was a instagram business trip.
the truth is
you can't see awe through a camera lens
or digital screen.
you can't buy a filter
or install an app
that will process awe for you
though you will try.
the awe you search for deep inside
the secret is hidden in your eyes
and processed by none other than your mind.
all you have to do
is put down your phone and try
the awe of the world
will open its gates
and break your perception of reality and
fiction.
a thousand colors
yet to be seen by human eye
that i will take over a screen any day.

THE OUTRO

THIS IS THE LAST STOP,

THOUGH I DO HOPE THAT YOUR TRAIN WILL CONTINUE ON.

LET THIS BOOK STAND

AS A CHANNEL TO DEEP DISCOVERY.

LET IT PROVOKE INTUITIVE THOUGHTS,

AND SPARK CREATIVE THINKING.

THE WILD WILL REMIND YOU

THAT YOUR TRUE COLORS ARE ALSO YOUR BEST.

BROKEN,

TO REMEMBER TEARS HAVE AND WILL BE SHED.

NEVER FORGET THE SACRIFICE

THE PEACEKEEPERS MADE FOR YOU,

OR HOW THE CHANGING OF SEASONS

IS SIMILAR TO THE CHANGING OF THOUGHTS AND ACTIONS.

THE LOVELY SIDE OF THINGS WILL ALWAYS BE LOVELY,

EVEN AS THE DARK COLD WORLD GRABS ONTO YOUR SHOULDERS.

IN THOSE DARK MOMENTS PLEASE REMEMBER

THAT NO MATTER HOW BAD IT GETS

THERE WILL ALWAYS BE HOPE,

EVEN IF THAT HARDLY MEANS A THING.

THERE WILL ALWAYS BE THOUGHTS

THAT HAVEN'T BEEN EXPLORED,

AND EXPLORATIONS THAT ARE WAITING FOR YOU.
AND WHEN YOU RETURN FROM YOUR ADVENTURES
NO MATTER WHAT SHAPE AND FORM,
REMEMBER TO WRITE THEM DOWN,
THEY MEAN SOMETHING TO SOMEONE SOMEWHERE.
SO SING, WRITE, DANCE,
PLAY, SLEEP, LOVE,
DO WHAT YOU HAVE TO,
MAKE THAT HEART DANCE TO A HAPPY BEAT.
DEAR READER,
I SAY THIS WITH INTENTIONAL THOUGHT AND
WITH A LOT OF CARE,
THERE WILL ALWAYS
BE A BETTER YOU
CHASING SOMETHING BETTER THAN
WHAT YOU ARE NOW,
AND YOU CAN'T STOP THAT
NO MATTER WHAT YOU FEEL ABOUT WHAT YOU HAVE
CURRENTLY,
EMBRACE YOUR FUTURE.
AND TEND TO IT WITH GREAT CARE.
FAREWELL READER,
I HOPE THE JOURNEY HAS BEEN SWELL,
BUT IT DOES END HERE, UNFORTUNATELY.
BEST WISHES TO YOU
AND TO THE STARS
AND TO THE WILD.

A long lost friend is coming home,
A happy faith of a six month old,
A deep blue sea and the world above,
The tingling mind of a girl in love,
And all the stories yet untold,
And all the stories yet untold.
The last three words of how you feel,
And all your dreams never made them real,
The money lost in a wishing well,
Teary taste of a kiss farewell,
And all the stories yet untold,
And all the stories yet untold.
If only I,
Could see your face,
Because that's when I can erase.
All the pain in your eyes,
Goes away in a beautiful surprise,
So the stories stay untold,
For the sake of our long lasting love.
And all the stories yet untold,
And all the stories yet untold.
And all the stories cannot stay untold,
And all the stories must be told.

endnote

you've made it out alive. and you always will. the battle is far from over, but you'll be just fine. we promise.

now go create and love and think and express and explore and wonder.

Go.

live.

The Poetry Book

Wild

Broken

Peacekeepers

Seasons

The 'Lovely' Side of Things

Dark Cold World

Hope

The Others

Poems Minus the Length

Prose

And Finally..